Cats Rule!

Cat CARE

Nutrition, Exercise, Grooming and More

by Carly J. Bacon

raintree

a Capstone company — publishers for children

Raintree is an imprint of Capstone Global Library Limited, a company incorporated in England and Wales having its registered office at 264 Banbury Road, Oxford, OX2 7DY – Registered company number: 6695582

www.raintree.co.uk
myorders@raintree.co.uk

Text © Capstone Global Library Limited 2017
The moral rights of the proprietor have been asserted.

Edited by Carrie Sheely, Alesha Halvorson
Designed by Philippa Jenkins
Illustrated by HL Studios p. 6, Jeff Edwards p. 14, F
Original illustrations © Capstone Global Library Lim
Picture research by Svetlana Zhurkin
Production by Steve Walker
Originated by Capstone Global Library Limited
Printed and bound in China

ISBN 978 1 4747 1287 3 (hardback)
19 18 17 16 15
10 9 8 7 6 5 4 3 2 1

ISBN 978 1 4747 1720 5 (paperback)
20 19 18 17
10 9 8 7 6 5 4 3 2

British Library Cataloguing in Publication Data
A full catalogue record for this book is available from the British Library.

Acknowledgements
We would like to thank the following for permission to reproduce photographs: Capstone Press: Philippa Jenkins, back cover and throughout, Karon Dubke, 28, 29; Dreamstime: Oscar Williams, 13; iStockphoto: MikaTrta, 11, RyersonClark, 25 (top); Shutterstock: Alena Ozerova, 5, Andrey_Kuzmin, 26, Drozdowski, 8, Eric Isselee, 14, Evgeny Karandaev, 7, Evgenyi, 6, 25 (bottom), IrinaK, 17 (bottom), Ivonne Wierink, 15, Lubava, 19, Michael Pettigrew, 23, MidoSemsem, 4, Natalya Onishchenko, 16, Okssi, cover, Oleksandr Schevchuk, 18, Sergey Gerashchenko, 24, Svetoslav Radkov, 17 (top), Tarapong Srichaiyos, 21, Volt Collection, 20, Yellowj, 22; Svetlana Zhurkin, 9

The author would like to thank Laurie Patton, Regional Director, TICA Southeast, for her invaluable help in the preparation of this book.

Some words are shown in bold, **like this**. You can find out what they mean by looking in the glossary.

Contents

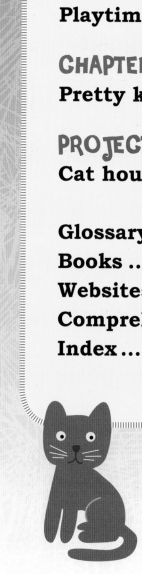

CHAPTER 1

Cat companions

If you love cats, you're in good company. More than 18 per cent of UK households include cats. A cat can become a friend and a beloved member of your family. But owning a pet is about more than just falling in love with beautiful markings and big eyes. It is a big responsibility. It's up to you to help your cat live a long, happy life. Are you up to the challenge?

Did you know?

Zzzz! Cats sleep an average of 13 to 14 hours each day.

Cats can be excellent pets and companions.

Nutrition is an important part of cat care. While fruit and vegetables are good for humans, they aren't a good idea for cats. That means no sneaking the brussels sprouts to your cat under the table! Many foods that people eat, such as onions, chocolate and grapes, can harm your cat.

Cats are meat-eaters, so a high-protein diet is important. But that doesn't mean they should share bites of your roast chicken. Never give human food to your cat unless your vet advises it. A high-quality cat food has the vitamins and nutrients your cat needs.

Cat food is available in both wet and dry form. Because wet food contains more water than dry food, it helps both nutrition and **hydration**. When choosing cat food, ask your vet for advice and read the nutritional labels. Look for food that's high in protein such as beef, lamb or chicken. The food should contain little or no filler such as wheat, soy or corn.

hydration drinking enough water to stay healthy

As your cat ages, its nutritional needs change. Kittens need more fat for healthy development. Adult cats should eat lower-calorie food to avoid becoming overweight. At the age of about seven, a cat needs food made especially for senior cats. Foods are also designed for cats with health issues such as kidney disease or allergies.

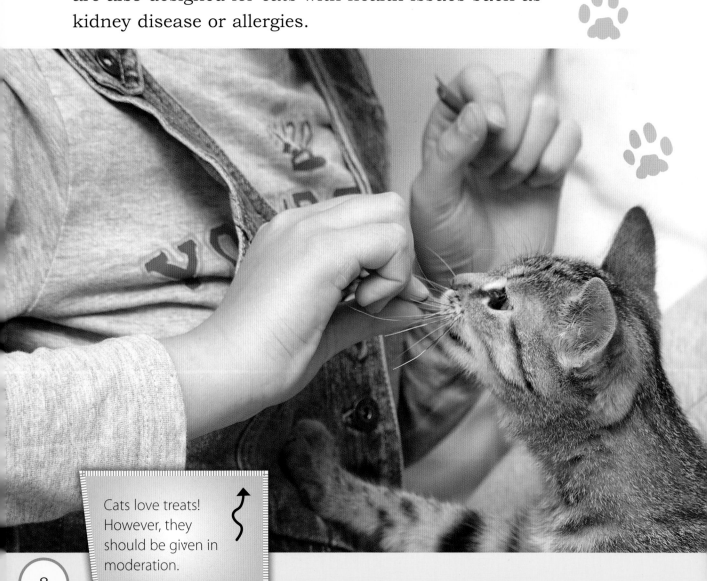

Cats love treats! However, they should be given in moderation.

Did you know?

Cats are famous for their love of milk. However, many cats are lactose intolerant and shouldn't be given milk. These cats have trouble digesting the sugar (lactose) in milk. It can cause an upset stomach.

Greenery and cats

Green plants are irresistible to many cats. But some plants are poisonous to them, including daffodil bulbs, oleander and poinsettias. Lilies are especially dangerous. When in doubt about whether a plant is safe, ask your vet. Signs that your cat may have eaten a poisonous plant include breathing difficulty, drooling, vomiting, diarrhoea and extreme thirst. If your cat has these symptoms, call your vet immediately.

Stay hydrated

Water is just as important for cats as it is for people. Water makes up 80 per cent of most cats' bodies. That sounds like a lot, doesn't it? A dehydrated cat can have problems with **circulation**, digestion and removing waste from its body.

Keep fresh water available to your cat at all times. You might want to get a pet drinking fountain, which keeps the water flowing, fresh and filtered. If you don't have a fountain, change the water daily. If your cat drinks more water than usual or is isn't drinking at all, it may be unwell. Check with your vet straight away.

Cat drinking fountains

You can buy a cat drinking fountain from some pet shops or online. You should buy a stainless steel or ceramic bowl for the fountain. Just like people, cats can get spots. Plastic bowls can be the cause.

circulation movement of blood through the body

Your cat's water bowl should be cleaned every day.

Exercise and diet

Studies show that up to 40 per cent of pet cats in the UK are overweight. Just like people, cats become overweight when they eat too much and exercise too little. Overweight cats are more likely to develop health problems such as **diabetes** and **arthritis**.

In the wild, cats eat about seven small meals a day. Some owners mimic this by leaving dry cat food out for their cats to nibble throughout the day. But some cats will eat all the food at once. These cats need to be put on a feeding schedule. Cats should be fed at least twice a day. An automated feeder can help you to stay on schedule if you can't be at home at feeding time.

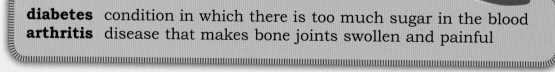

diabetes condition in which there is too much sugar in the blood
arthritis disease that makes bone joints swollen and painful

Regular visits to the vet can help determine your cat's best feeding schedule.

Some cat breeds naturally weigh more than others. For example, male Maine Coon cats can weigh up to 8 kilograms (18 pounds). On the other hand, male Singapuras average 2.5 to 3 kilograms (6 to 7 pounds). Ask your vet about your cat's ideal weight and how much food you should feed it.

If your cat is overweight, ask your vet how to help it lose weight in a healthy way. If a cat loses weight too quickly, it can cause life-threatening liver problems. Cats that stop eating completely can fall ill very quickly. Call your vet straight away if your cat isn't eating.

Maine Coons (below) reach their full size between the ages of three and five years old.

Did you know?

The heaviest domestic cat on record weighed 21.2 kilograms (46.8 pounds)! Himmy lived in Australia and died at the age of ten.

Checking kitty's weight

Feel your cat's ribs and then look down at its body from above. Your cat is at a healthy weight if you can slightly feel the ribs and if it has a slight waist when viewed from above. If your cat's ribs are very easy to feel and it has a pronounced waist, your cat is underweight. An overweight cat's ribs are difficult to feel. It has either no visible waist or its body curves outwards at the middle.

CHAPTER 3

Playtime!

The second part of keeping your cat fit and healthy is regular exercise. You may notice that your cat gets bursts of energy during certain times of the day. Pay attention to your cat's habits and make the most of these playful spurts. Playing is important for your cat's health and can be fun for both of you.

Different cats prefer different types of play. Notice what your cat responds to best. Also, your cat's likes and dislikes may change as it ages. An old cat may not have as much energy or motivation to play as a younger cat. You may need to get creative when encouraging an older cat to play.

crepuscular active during twilight

Get your cat moving with a game of chase-and-fetch with a small ball.

Did you know?

Cats are crepuscular, which means they are most active at dawn and dusk. Has your cat ever tried to wake you up to play at the crack of dawn?

A wand toy allows for some distance between your skin and your cat's claws!

🐾 Toys for cats

Just like children, cats need toys. But cat toys don't have to be expensive or high-tech. A paper bag on the floor can entertain a cat for a long time. Remove any handles on the bag, which could choke your cat. Many cats can't resist jumping into a cardboard box. Table tennis balls and empty cardboard toilet rolls are also items that your cat may enjoy.

When you're at home, join in to make playtime more exciting. Tap the back of a paper bag to grab your cat's interest. Or drag a ribbon around the house for your cat to chase. Make sure you supervise your cat, though. Ribbon and wool can be choking hazards. Never let your cat play with plastic bags. Cats can suffocate in these bags.

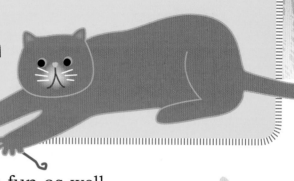
Toys from pet shops can be fun as well. Make toys move like a cat's natural **prey**. When they're outside, cats chase birds, mice and insects. A laser pointer mimics a flying insect. Try making a small stuffed animal on a string bounce like a hopping rabbit. Make a ribbon slither like a snake. Be sure to let your cat "win" these games. A cat may lose interest if it never catches the fake prey.

Your cat may like different coloured or textured toys.

prey animal hunted by another animal for food

CHAPTER 4

Pretty kitties and spa days

For everyday grooming, cats get a gold star. If a cat has ever licked your hand, you know how rough its tongue is. Cats' tongues help them remove dirt and dead fur. They also help to spread natural oils, called **sebum**, through a cat's fur. By grooming with its tongue, a cat helps its coat stay shiny, waterproof and tangle-free. Grooming even helps cats to stay cool. When they cover their fur with saliva, their body temperatures drop as the saliva evaporates. Cats can't sweat as much as humans do, and they don't usually pant like dogs.

Did you know?

If a cat does pant, it could be a sign of illness. Call your vet for help.

Cats have their own built-in grooming tools – their tongues and teeth.

Although cats do a good job of cleaning themselves, they should be brushed with a pet brush at least once a week. This helps reduce shedding and prevent **furballs**. If your cat has long hair, you'll need to brush it every day. Furballs can cause vomiting and constipation. If furballs become a problem even with regular brushing, consider feeding your cat a food made to prevent furballs.

Brushing your cat removes dirt, grease, dead hair and dead skin from its coat.

sebum oily liquid produced by glands in the skin
furball ball of fur that lodges in a cat's stomach

Home-made shampoo

Never use shampoo for humans on your cat. Cat shampoo is available at pet shops. You can also make your own cat shampoo by mixing these ingredients in a clean bottle:

- 235 millilitres (1 cup) white or apple vinegar
- 235 millilitres (1 cup) natural (organic) washing-up liquid
- 945 millilitres (4 cup) water

 ## Bath time

It's usually not necessary to bathe cats, which is a good thing. Most cats aren't big fans of getting wet! However, cats can sometimes get into messes bigger than their grooming skills can handle. If your cat gets into something that's very dirty or sticky, it may need a bath.

Cat baths are generally a two-person job, so ask an adult to help. You can bathe your cat in a sink or bath. Make sure you use lukewarm water. Have a large, fluffy towel near by. The first step is to pour the water gently over your cat with a cup or jug. Be careful to avoid the cat's eyes, ears and nose. Once the fur is wet, gently lather with a shampoo made for cats. Then carefully rinse until all the soap is out. You may need to rinse more than once.

If your cat's face is dirty, wipe it gently with a damp flannel. Don't use shampoo near your cat's face, because it may get into its eyes. To dry, wrap your cat in the towel and gently massage its fur. When you've finished, praise your cat and give it a treat.

After a bath praise your cat with its favourite treat.

Feline feet!

Cats scratch to mark their territories, strengthen muscles and reduce stress. To prevent damage to curtains and furniture, keep your cat's claws clipped. Regular claw clipping also reduces accidental scratches during playtime. A cat's claws must be trimmed correctly with a clipper made especially for cats. This can be tricky, and you should always ask an adult for help. Cat trees or Scratching posts give your cat appropriate places to use their claws.

In some countries, people choose to declaw their cats' front paws. Declawing is banned in the UK and many other European countries. There are many reasons to not declaw your cat. It can affect a cat's balance and make it less able to survive if it gets lost outside. Many vets won't carry out the procedure because they consider it to be invasive. It involves removing bone so that the claws won't grow back.

Dental care

If your cat has plaque, receding gums or is drooling, it may have gum disease or tooth decay. Your vet can clean your cat's teeth, but it can be expensive and unpleasant for your cat. Regular dental care is important. Get your cat used to having its teeth brushed when it is a kitten. You can buy cat toothpaste and toothbrushes at pet shops or online.

 ## Cat ID

A cat may wander off and get lost. A tag with the cat's name and your contact information on its collar will help return your cat to you. Some owners ask their vet to put a microchip in their cats. If a microchipped cat gets lost, a vet or the RSPCA can retrieve your contact information by scanning the microchip.

Cleaning Up!

While cleaning the litterbox is a necessary task if your cat lives indoors, it isn't much fun. If you use clumping litter, scoop out the clumps of waste every day. If you use crystal, clay or any other type of non-clumping litter, you'll need to change the litter about every other day. Try to use the same kind of litter all the time. Your cat may not like different types of litter or be upset by the change.

Cats are less likely to urinate around the house if the litter tray is clean. Cats are more sensitive to smells than humans. If you can smell the tray, just think about how bad it smells to your cat. That's a good reason not to use a covered litter tray. Covered litter trays trap the odour inside. They also may not give your cat much room to move around.

Did you know?

If your cat suddenly stops using its litter tray, it could be a sign of illness such as a urinary tract infection or kidney or liver issues. Call your vet immediately.

 ## Check-ups

Annual vet visits are important for your cat. Check-ups and vaccines are necessary to prevent illness and to spot any health issues. Vaccines are important to keep your cat from developing fatal diseases such as **feline distemper** and rabies.

All owners should have their cats spayed or neutered. As well as preventing unwanted kittens, spaying or neutering your cat has many other benefits. Unneutered male cats are much more likely to mark their territories by spraying urine in the house. Spaying and neutering also helps protect cats against cancer of the breast and reproductive organs.

feline distemper serious and sometimes fatal cat disease that involves fever, vomiting, diarrhoea and dehydration

Cat house and bed

Treat your cat to its own house and bed. Get creative, but be sure to use materials without small pieces that could be a choking hazard. When you've finished, watch your cat investigate the house. Some cats need time to adjust to a new item. Give your cat the space and time it needs to explore.

What you need:

- cardboard box large enough for your cat to turn around in
- utility knife
- 2 pieces of fleece fabric, large enough to fit inside the box.
- ruler
- masking tape
- fabric scissors
- pillow stuffing
- felt-tip pens or scraps of fabric

What to do:

1. Ask an adult to help you cut a hole in the side of the box with the utility knife. The hole should be large enough for your cat to enter and exit freely.

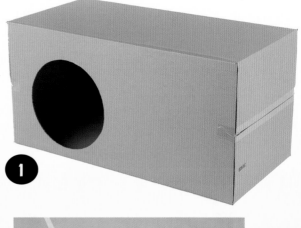

2. Put the two pieces of fleece fabric together so that the edges line up.

3. Measure 10 centimetres (4 in.) in from each edge of the fabric and mark with masking tape.

28

4. With the scissors, cut 2.5-cm (1-in.) strips along the edges of your fabric up to the masking tape. This creates fringe on all four sides.

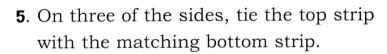

5. On three of the sides, tie the top strip with the matching bottom strip.

6. Use the open side to stuff the pillow stuffing into the cat bed.

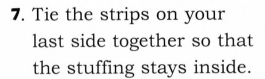

8. Remove masking tape.

7. Tie the strips on your last side together so that the stuffing stays inside.

9. Place the bed inside the closed box for your cat.

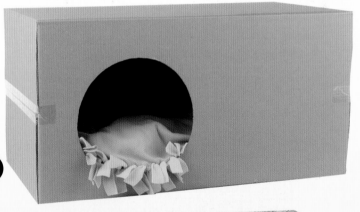

10. Decorate the box with felt-tip pens. You could even get creative with different fabrics on the outside of the box.

Glossary

arthritis disease that makes bone joints swollen and painful

circulation movement of blood through the body

crepuscular active during twilight

diabetes condition in which there is too much sugar in the blood

feline distemper serious and sometimes fatal cat disease that involves fever, vomiting, diarrhoea and dehydration

furball ball of fur that lodges in a cat's stomach

hydration drinking enough water to stay healthy

prey animal hunted by another animal for food

sebum oily liquid produced by glands in the skin

Books

Care for your Kitten (RSPCA Pet Guide), RSPCA (HarperCollins, 2015)

Caring for Cats and Kittens (Battersea Dogs & Cats Home Pet Care Guides), Ben Hubbard (Franklin Watts, 2015)

Cool Cat Projects (Pet Projects) Isabel Thomas (Raintree, 2015)

Looking after Cats and Kittens, Katherine Starke (Usborne Publishing Ltd, 2013)

 # Websites

www.cats.org.uk/cat-care/cats-for-kids

Find out some fascinating feline facts, take part in fun activities and games and get useful cat care advice.

www.rspca.org.uk/adviceandwelfare/pets/cats

Find out more about cat behaviour.

Comprehension questions

1. What items are dangerous for cats to play with unsupervised? Why?

2. Why do you think there are so many overweight cats?

3. What are the advantages of owning a cat rather than other types of pet? Are there any disadvantages to owning a cat?

Index